THINKABOUT

Smelling

Text: Henry Pluckrose
Photography: Chris Fairclough

Watts Books
London • New York • Sydney

The world is
full of things
to smell -
some pleasant...

and some horrid.

Think of all these different smells – ripe fruit…

fresh bread…

strong cheese…

hot pizza…

shampoos, bath oils
and perfumes…

leather and polish…

and petrol
at the garage.

In the garden
you might smell
the sweet scent
of flowers...

the earthiness
of dead leaves
or wet soil...

the heavy scent
of cut grass.

In cities,
we live with
the stale fumes
of cars and lorries...

and the reek of smoke from factories.

Not all smells
are pleasant.
Have you smelled
stinking waste
pouring into the sea?

Have you smelled a field being sprayed…

or the sourness
of dirty water?

What things do you most like
to smell -
the saltiness of the sea…

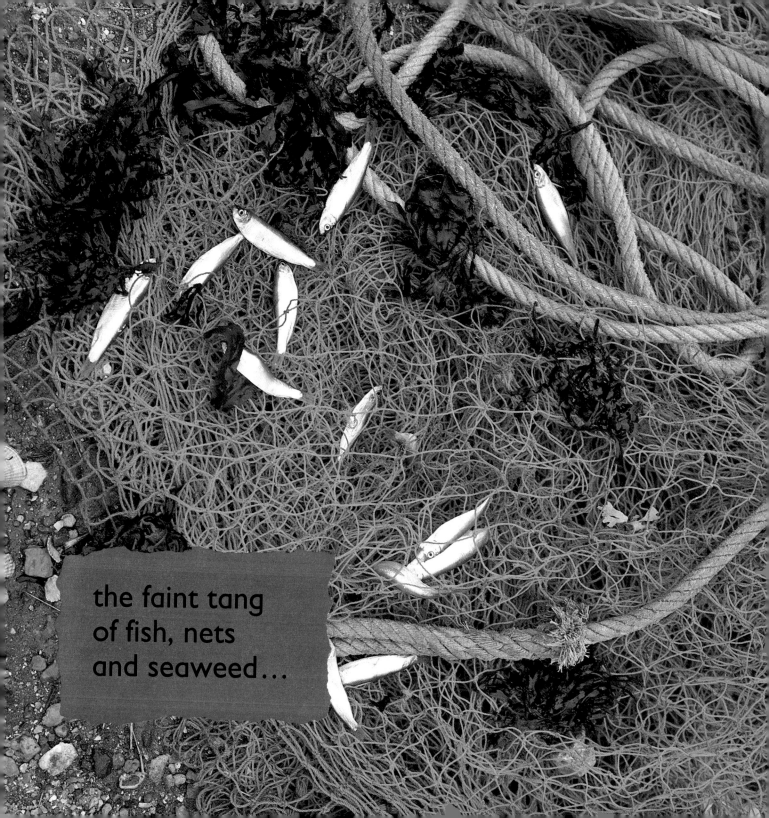

the faint tang
of fish, nets
and seaweed…

newly-cut wood...

the fresh smell
of shampoo...

or ironed clothes?

Which food smells tempt you more - steaming apple pie...

or baked potato
with melting butter?

Which do
you think
smells nicer -
flowers...

or fruity soaps?
What is your
favourite smell?

About this book

This book is designed for use in the home, playgroup, kindergarten and infant school.

Parents can share the book with young children. Its aim is to bring into focus some of the elements of life and living which are all too often taken for granted. To develop fully, all young children need to have their understanding of the world deepened and the language they use to express their ideas extended. This book, and others in the series, takes the everyday things of the child's world and explores them, harnessing curiosity and wonder in a purposeful way.

For those working with young children each book is designed to be used both as a picture book, which explores ideas and concepts, and as a starting point to talk and exploration. The pictures have been selected because they are of interest in themselves and also because they include elements which will promote enquiry. Talk can lead to displays of items and pictures collected by children and teacher. Pictures and collages can be made by the children themselves.

Everything in our environment is of interest to the growing child. The purpose of these books is to extend and develop that interest.

Henry Pluckrose